WOW
WORLD OF WONDER

I didn't know that

Get ready to hear your kids say, "Wow! I didn't know that!" as they dive into this fun, informative, question-answering series of books! Students—and teachers and parents—will learn things about the world around them that they never knew before!

This approach to education seeks to promote an interest in learning by answering questions kids have always wondered about. When books answer questions that kids already want to know the answers to, kids love to read those books, fostering a love for reading and learning, the true keys to lifelong education.

Colorful graphics are labeled and explained to connect with visual learners, while in-depth explanations of each subject will connect with those who prefer reading or listening as their learning style.

This educational series makes learning fun through many levels of interaction. The in-depth information combined with fantastic illustrations promote learning and retention, while question and answer boxes reinforce the subject matter to promote higher order thinking.

Teachers and parents love this series because it engages young people, sparking an interest and desire in learning. It doesn't feel like work to learn about a new subject with books this interactive and interesting.

This set of books will be an addition to your home or classroom library that everyone will enjoy. And, before you know it, you, too, will be saying, "Wow! I didn't know that!"

"People cannot learn by having information pressed into their brains. Knowledge has to be sucked into the brain, not pushed in. First, one must create a state of mind that craves knowledge, interest, and wonder. You can teach only by creating an urge to know." - Victor Weisskopf

© 2012 Flowerpot Press

Contents under license from Aladdin Books Ltd.

Flowerpot Press
142 2nd Avenue North
Franklin, TN 37064

Flowerpot Press is a division of Kamalu, LLC,
Franklin, TN, U.S.A.,
and Mitso Media, Inc., Oakville, ON, Canada.

ISBN 978-1-77093-776-5

Concept, editorial, and design by
David West Children's Books

Designer:
Robert Perry

Illustrators:
James Field - Simon Girling and Associates
Mike Lacy
Jo Moore

American Edition Editor:
Johannah Gilman Paiva

American Redesign:
Jonas Fearon Bell

Printed in China.

WORLD OF WONDER

WOW

WORLD OF WONDER

I didn't know that

dinosaurs

laid

eggs

I didn't know that

Introduction

Did you know that some dinosaurs had feathers? That some could fly? That there were real sea monsters in dinosaur times?

Discover for yourself amazing facts about prehistoric life, how big the animals were, what they ate, how their babies were born, and how we know all this.

 Watch for this symbol, which means there is a fun project for you to try.

 True or False? Watch for this symbol and try to answer the question before reading on for the answer.

I didn't know that

all dinosaurs died out 65 million years ago. For 150 million years, Earth was a planet inhabited by dinosaurs—until disaster struck. Maybe a meteorite hit the Earth, or maybe a large number of volcanoes erupted, but the dinosaurs were no more.

We know about dinosaurs because people have discovered their fossilized remains in rocks. Fossil specialists, or paleontologists, can piece fossils together and figure out how the dinosaurs lived.

True or False?
Humans were responsible for making the dinosaurs extinct.

Answer: **False**
Humans and dinosaurs never lived together on Earth. Over 60 million years separate the last dinosaurs and our earliest ancestors.

One Million Years B.C.—films that got it wrong!

Saltasaurus

Dinosaur history is divided into three periods: Triassic (early), Jurassic (middle), and Cretaceous (late). Different dinosaurs lived in different periods.

Coelophysis

Stegosaurus

Tyrannosaurus

Triassic

Jurassic

Cretaceous

! **Crocodiles have barely changed at all since dinosaur times.**

I didn't know that

dinosaur means "terrible lizard." By 1841, people realized that these enormous fossilized bones belonged to huge extinct reptiles, not giant humans! Scientist Dr. Richard Owen named them "dino" (terrible) "saurs" (lizards).

One of the differences between dinosaurs and other reptile families, such as crocodiles or lizards, is that dinosaurs walked on straight legs.

A dinosaur's skin would have been very tough and scaly to the touch. Like a snake's skin, which people sometimes expect to be slimy, it would have felt dry and bumpy.

Thirty-nine feet (almost 12 meters) tall with a three-foot (almost one meter) wide mouth, and teeth as long as carving knives, Tyrannosaurus rex was a nightmare lizard! Its name means "King Tyrant Lizard."

Close-up of T. rex's skin

T. rex's fossilized tooth

The first dinosaur discovered in the West was found in 1824.

I didn't know that

some dinosaurs were bigger than a four-story building. Ultrasaurus was a huge sauropod, the biggest dinosaur ever at 98 feet (almost 30 meters) long and 39 feet (almost 12 meters) high. A human would barely have reached its ankles!

Can you find nine Compsognathuses?

Fossilized footprints show that the enormous sauropods moved in groups, walking with long strides. Some might have swum across rivers, pulling themselves along with their front legs.

The chicken-sized Compsognathus was one of the smallest dinosaurs. It was a speedy meat-eater, which chased after tiny mammals, lizards, and insects.

Mamenchisaurus had a 33 foot (10 meter) long neck!

I didn't know that

some dinosaurs hunted in packs. Fossils have been found of a group of Deinonychuses surrounding a Tenontosaurus, an herbivore. They probably hunted together, like lions or wolves.

Deinonychus

Deinonychus had long claws for stabbing and cutting. On each hind foot, it had a special slashing claw, which could be pulled back when it ran.

A hug from Deinocheirus, "terrible hand," would have been deadly! Its arms were over eight feet (2.4 meters) long. This birdlike creature was probably bigger than T. rex.

Deinocheirus

Tenontosaurus

All meat-eating dinosaurs were theropods, with three toes and long claws. Most walked on two legs.

Apatosaurus

I didn't know that

most dinosaurs ate plants. The earliest dinosaurs were meat-eaters, but by the Jurassic period, plant-eaters were flourishing. There was still no grass to graze on—instead they grazed on other plants.

Sauropods—like Diplodocus and Apatosaurus had teeth—like pegs for raking leaves, or spoon-shaped ones for pulling leaves off a plant. They swallowed without chewing.

Big plant-eating dinosaurs had to eat 400 pounds of leaves a day!

Hadrosaurs (duckbills like Parasaurolophus and Edmontosaurus) could eat Christmas trees! They ground twigs and pine needles between jaws that contained more than a thousand teeth pressed together into ridged plates.

Scientists can also learn about dinosaur diets from their fossilized droppings, which might contain seeds, leaves, or fish scales.

Ceratopsian dinosaurs (like Centrosaurus) had parrot-like beaks for cropping very tough plants, and strong jaws and sharp teeth for cutting them up.

I didn't know that

some dinosaurs went fishing. Baryonyx, "heavy claw," was discovered in 1983. It had unusually long, curved claws and a fossilized fish in its stomach. Scientists thought the claws were used for hooking fish out of the water.

Millions of years after the crime, a fossilized Oviraptor, "egg thief," was caught! It had a telltale pair of prongs in its otherwise toothless mouth. They were probably used for cracking the eggs it stole.

True or False?
Some dinosaurs had no teeth at all.

Answer: **True**
The birdlike Gallimimus, an ornithopod, had no teeth. Twice the size of an ostrich, it fed on insects and anything it could swallow whole.

Like snakes, dinosaurs also swallowed a meal without chewing. The fossilized skeleton of a Compsognathus (see page 11) was discovered with a whole, fossilized lizard in its stomach.

I didn't know that

dinosaurs laid eggs. They did—just like all reptiles. The dinosaur mother would scrape out a hollow nest in the ground and cover the eggs to keep them warm. She would bring food to her babies until they could leave the nest.

True or False?
The biggest dinosaurs laid giant eggs more than three feet (1 meter) long.

Can you find the imposter?

Answer: **False**
Even the biggest dinosaur eggs were no more than five times the size of a chicken's egg. A bigger egg would need to have a thicker shell, which would suffocate the baby.

Fossilized footprints of small tracks surrounded by larger ones show that young dinosaurs on the move were protected by the older, larger ones.

! Like a cuckoo, the Troodon may have laid its eggs in others' nests.

I didn't know that

some dinosaurs were armor-plated. This was protection from the fierce meat-eaters, such as Carnotaurus, that hunted them. Like armadillos and porcupines today, certain plant-eaters had tough skins or spikes.

Carnotaurus

Euoplocephalus

Euoplocephalus even had bony eyelids! It also had spikes and a lethal clubbed tail for defense—enough to make any predator think twice.

20

Sauropods were protected by sheer size, but a group of Triceratops could make a wall of horns that would scare off their enemies.

Tyrannosaurus rex

Triceratops

True or False?
The spiny plates on a Stegosaurus (right) were for protection.

Answer: **False**
They were probably for controlling its body heat. Blood so near the skin's surface could warm up very quickly in the sun, or cool down in the shade.

! **Diplodocus used its tail as a defensive whip.**

I didn't know that

some dinosaurs had head-butting contests. Like rams and stags today, "boneheads," such as Stegoceras, battled for leadership. Their skulls were 10 inches (25 centimeters) thick, so it probably didn't hurt very much.

Some duck-billed dinosaurs, like Parasaurolophus, had hollow headpieces that were connected to their nasal passages. They might have snored! They didn't use their crests for fighting head-to-head.

Can you find the chameleon?

No one knows what colors dinosaurs were. Like reptiles and birds today, they were probably colored to blend in with their surroundings. Like chameleons, some might have changed color.

I didn't know that

Quetzalcoatlus was bigger than a hang glider. With a wingspan of 32 feet (almost 10 meters), it was the biggest creature ever to take to the air, gliding on warm air currents. Flying reptiles were not dinosaurs, but pterosaurs.

Dimorphodon

Rhamphorhynchus

Pteranodon

True or False?
Pterosaurs had feathers.

Answer: False
More like bats than birds, pterosaurs like Dimorphodon had furry bodies and leathery wings. They had beaked faces, but they also had teeth.

The winged dinosaur, Archaeopteryx, was probably the first bird.

Quetzalcoatlus

Pteranodon swooped down from the cliff tops to catch fish from the sea. The crest on its head helped it to steer.

Pterodaustro also ate fish. It had a sieve in its beak so it could strain tiny fish as it flew low over the water.

I didn't know that

there were real sea monsters in dinosaur times. Dinosaurs didn't live in the sea, but it was full of all sorts of other huge and strange-looking swimming reptiles. They fed on fish and shellfish.

Elasmosaurus

The plesiosaur Elasmosaurus was 50 feet (15 meters) long, and nearly all neck. Swimming through the water, it must have looked like Diplodocus with flippers!

! The turtle-like Archelon was longer than a rowboat.

❗ Some think the Loch Ness Monster may be a plesiosaur.

Ichthyosaurs were some of the earliest sea reptiles. They looked like dolphins and, like dolphins, breathed air. They fed on the ammonites and belemnites often found as fossils today.

Ichthyosaurs

Liopleurodon was one of the short-necked plesiosaurs. It really was a monster—its head was seven feet (over two meters) long!

Mosasaurus

Liopleurodon

Mosasaurs were some of the last sea reptiles and, at 33 feet (10 meters) long, the largest lizards ever. They looked like dragons, but with flippers rather than legs.

I didn't know that

some dinosaurs had feathers. A fossil of a feathered dinosaur was found in China in 1996. New discoveries can change the way we think about dinosaurs. Just imagine how different they would look with feathers!

 Paleontologists piece together dinosaur bones into skeletons, then flesh out the skeletons. They have to guess the colors. Take your own dinosaur models and paint them. What colors will you choose and why?

Close-up
view of
feathers

Mosasaurs were some
of the last sea reptiles
and, at 33 feet (10
meters) long, the largest
lizards ever. They looked
like dragons, but with
flippers rather than legs.

Even though
the feathers
were probably
for warmth rather
than for flying, this
find makes it even
more likely that
modern birds are
related to dinosaurs.

Glossary

Ammonites
Prehistoric shellfish, commonly found as fossils.

Belemnites
Prehistoric bull-shaped shellfish, also common fossils.

Boneheads
The nickname given to Pachycephalosaurus. They were two-legged dinosaurs with incredibly thick skulls.

Ceratopsians
Dinosaurs that had horns and a protective bony frill.

Fossils
The remains of living things that have been preserved in rock.

Hadrosaurs
Duck-billed dinosaurs, often with a crest on their head.

Herbivore
Any plant-eater.

Ichthyosaurs
Dolphin-like sea reptiles that lived at the same time as dinosaurs.

Mosasaurs
Dragon-like sea reptiles that lived at the same time as dinosaurs.

Ornithopods

A group of dinosaurs that walked on two legs. Most were herbivores.

Paleontologists

Scientists who study the fossilized remains of extinct animals and plants.

Plesiosaurs

Sea reptiles, with flippers rather than legs, that lived at the same time as dinosaurs.

Pterosarus

A group of flying reptiles that lived at the same time as dinosaurs.

Sauropods

A group of long-necked, long-tailed, four-legged, plant-eating dinosaurs. They included Diplodocus and Apatosaurus.

Theropods

A group of meat-eating dinosaurs. Most of them walked on two legs. They included Deinonychus.

Index